Published by Bloomsbury Publishing, New York and London
Distributed to the trade by Holtzbrinck Publishers

All papers used by Bloomsbury Publishing are natural, recyclable products made from wood grown in well-managed forests. The manufacturing processes conform to the environmental regulations of the country of origin.

Library of Congress Cataloging-in-Publication Data has been applied for.

ISBN 1-59691-048-8
ISBN-13 978-1-59691-048-5

First U.S. Edition 2005

1 3 5 7 9 10 8 6 4 2

Printed and bound in Italy by Graphicom

FOREWORD BY
David Hockney

I don't know anything about Denys Dawnay, but I'm sure I would have liked him. He has an attitude to style, his drawings are beautiful and his drawings of drawings exceptional, particularly his Holbein drawings – even the head gear fits perfectly. And he loved dachshunds. What a combination: dachshunds and painting (in a future life I wouldn't mind being a dachshund in California).

Here is the work of a dachshund lover who has observed their habits and movements and indeed expressions for a long period. He was twenty-four when he made this book and he seems to me to get everything right. I have observed that these dogs want food and love in that order, which is of course just like us. 'Stomach above everything,' is a truthful motto for them. Anyone who has had the pleasure of living with dachshunds knows they are warm and essentially comic characters.

The joy here is in the love of dachshunds and a very good knowledge of pictures and their varieties of style. Is it the whole picture you see first, or the dachshund? Sometimes I'm not sure, but that's the delight of the book for me.

Lucinda Lambton

Denys Dawnay was as delicate as the dachshunds that he drew, and every bit as remarkable. Although a frail, pale figure who was chronically ill throughout his life with severe diabetes – as well as being struck down for years with tuberculosis – he nevertheless produced a volume of exquisite and varied work: paintings, drawings, cartoons, models and photographs, as well as poetry and prose.

This book, written and painted when he was only twenty-four years old, was given to my parents Bindy and Tony Lambton in 1945, after he had stayed with them for many months during the war. Growing especially fond of their black and tan dachshund, Flower, he was given to fantastical musings about the dog's noble yet notorious ancestry. So the idea for *The House of Tekelden* was born.

It is a book that is as curious as it is clever, as rare as it is beautiful, with every turn of the page making you laugh out loud with surprise and delight. From the weavers of the Bayeux Tapestry to the paintbrushes of Picasso, as well as Van Eyck, Holbein, Gainsborough and Whistler – to name but a few – Denys gets them all to tackle the Tekeldens, and his exquisite parodies of their masterpieces are little masterpieces in themselves.

For my sisters, my brother and me as children, this was our introduction to the history of art, but as we eagerly followed the family's progress down the centuries we never suspected how much we were learning. We were thrilled to see the sinister armies of 'Rattila the Hund' silhouetted against the flames during the sack of Rome in 463. It seemed quite plausible to us that Jan Tekelden, painted by Van Eyck, should be immortalised by Chaucer in his poem 'The Rat's Tail'. Most fascinating of all to our childish taste was 'The Beast … Odo Tekelden, Cardinal Lord Archbishop of Bavaria, known as Odo the Odious' who had 'a most horrible dungeon in his castle, full of instruments of torture such as paw-pressers, ear- and nose-clippers and tail-twisters'.

We grew up loving the beauty of Katherine Paw, wife of Heinrich Tekelden, who looked suspiciously like Henry VIII, and surely every child knew that Sir Walter Ratleigh – once Tekelden – had been knighted by Queen Elizabeth after casting his cloak in the mud in front of her lady-in-waiting? Then there was Ratbrandt Teckelden, the world-famous painter, and Carl Teckelden, 'The Snob', who was favoured by Charles II. It was he, according to Denys Dawnay, who was so horribly proud that he would sneer at his fellow dachshunds, quoting Pope's famous couplet 'I am his Highness' dog at Kew, Pray, tell me, Sir, whose dog are you?'

David Rattick the dachshund, who first drew our youthful attention to the paintings of Zoffany, was more familiar to us than David Garrick the actor. And then there was the cautionary tale of the 'The Rake', Flush Tekelden, who spent his fortune on gambling and gluttony. He married Madame Rattier, who was painted by David, and then, to restore his misspent fortune, 'Miss Ratschild of the great banking house'. His disgraceful words 'A dachshund can jog along on 40,000 pork pies year' were taken from the lips of our own great-great-great grandfather, 'Radical Jack' John George Lambton, the liberal reformer, who unwisely declared that 'A man can jog along on £40,000 a year.'

As far as I can discover, Denys produced four more books: another two of dachshunds for my mother and father, one for Lord and Lady Salisbury about their bull terrier, and another, it is rumoured, of corgis, for the royal family, who for over thirty years played an extraordinarily intimate role in his life, as he did in theirs.

Denys was born in 1921, the son of Colonel Alan Dawnay, who was celebrated by his friend T.E. Lawrence in *The Seven Pillars of Wisdom*. Denys went to Westminster School and then on to the Euston Road Art School, where he was taught by Victor Passmore. He later moved to Oxford, where he had a studio in the house that was alleged to have been lived in by Vanbrugh during the building of Blenheim, and fitfully attended the Ruskin School of Drawing which, during the Second World War, was merged with the Slade and set up in the Ashmolean Museum. It was in Oxford, whilst painting mainly portraits – his canvas of A.L. Rowse, done in 1942, is in the National Portrait Gallery – that he made an immense circle of friends, including my parents.

Sickly since early childhood with diabetes, Denys had to inject himself with insulin – more often than not plunging the needle straight through his trousers – three times a day. He stopped growing when still young, and thereafter his slender form, with his heavily bespectacled face (he was repeatedly told that he was going to go blind) had all the appearance of a fifteen-year-old. His bravery, however, was renowned. Rightly thinking that he might die any day, and constantly feeling both dizzy and queasy, he never complained, but instead was the whiplash wit of whatever company he kept. He made his companions howl with laughter at his every turn of phrase – often interrupted by having to rush out of the room to be violently sick – and all delivered in an oddly half-broken, high-pitched and very slow Edwardian drawl. I can still hear its strangely musical cadence today.

He was plagued, too, by diabetic comas; my parents once managed, in the nick of time, to save his life by stuffing rabbit food – all they could find that was edible – down his throat. Forever trying to stabilise his condition, he nevertheless drank heavily, and refused to eat the right food, except for the recommended daily glass of orange juice, which he insisted should have two teaspoons of sugar. His insulin levels, of course, went haywire. He smoked from dawn till dusk – often with a cigarette holder – and one of the few memories that I have of Denys is the brightness of his nicotine-stained fingers against the marble-like whiteness of the rest of his skin.

Home for him was both in London and at Ardgowan, a great eighteenth-century house in Renfrewshire, lived in by his mother Elizabeth Dawnay and his uncle, who later became his stepfather, Sir Guy Shaw-Stewart. Denys's aunt, Diana Shaw-Stewart, had died in 1931 shortly after giving birth to her fifth child, his beloved cousin Houston, and his mother had stepped in to look after her sister's children. So it was that Denys found himself living in the house where he had spent many childhood holidays and it was here that he would write and paint all his enchanting books. Poring over his work, in a large and rather dark room, with nineteenth-century flowered wallpaper, surrounded by easels and by cupboards bursting with paintings and paint, he would work away all day, talking to his giant green parrot, accompanied by either jazz or classical music.

In the early 1950s, while staying at Hatfield, Denys met Princess Margaret and thereafter his life was streamlined into a close friendship with the royal family that was to last until the end of his life. Throughout the fifties, sixties and seventies and until he died in 1983, he stayed for months at a time at Windsor, Balmoral and Sandringham, often with no other guests, and the albums that he kept of those visits, show that enormous pleasure was given on both sides.

In 1956 the Queen taught him to ride, patiently and alone in the riding school, with Denys 'on a very quiet pony called Caravan'; and that same year at Windsor, Denys bought the Duke of Edinburgh a paint-box for Christmas and began to teach him to paint. He and Prince Philip also made a wooden model of Balmoral, 'with the maximum amount of chaos and noise from the electric fretsaw, lathe and revolving sanding machine'. They made model aeroplanes too, and they painted posters for such events as Queen Elizabeth's Sale of Work at which the royal family and Denys manned the stalls. A 'Treasure Hunt' with his and Prince Philip's illustrations was such a success that the whole family wrote a letter of thanks to Denys, who, as was not uncommon, was ill in bed. There were hiccups: 'Having pestered to be allowed to drive the car,' wrote Denys of the Queen's Landrover, 'and boasted that I was the best driver in Scotland … I drove it straight off the road, hitting three trees and smashing all one side.' He had a mournful photograph taken of himself with his battered trophy.

Whereas many of us dream of a life of luxury, with our every need taken care of twenty-fours a day, for the invalid Denys this was sometimes no idle wish but a necessity. He often stayed in grand houses, which, in those austere war-time and post-war years, were the only houses able to accommodate the cosseting that he needed. A guest who stays in bed for six weeks on end, as Denys did at Balmoral, is not a guest that most households could take in their stride without flinching.

Life with the royal family was surely as perfect for Denys as his friendship was perfect for them. His physical condition may also have eased his singular path in another way, making him a unique addition to their lives: not even Prince Philip's passion for outdoor activities could be expected to apply to Denys. His physical frailty must have made him special, an exception to all the rules, even the rules of protocol.

He posed no threat and was no toad, but rather was their best friend, the best company that anyone could have ever had, providing wit, artistry, bohemianism and fun. Again and again, I have been told that no one else could make people laugh in the same uproarious way.

The photographs of Denys with the royal family are a testimony of what exceptionally happy times they had together. They would all go to the theatre and have supper in his modest London flat, where 'Prince Philip did the cooking.' Never boring and never bored, Denys was constantly interesting and inventive; organising plays for the family to perform, photographing, painting, even 'playing red Indians' and cooking drop scones on the new fangled barbecue that had been given as a present by Douglas Fairbanks. Despite Denys' rather effete figure seeming forever to be sitting in a chair, with a cocktail and a cigarette in a holder, he in fact galvanised all around him into action.

And he also galvanised himself. In the 1960s, when told yet again that he had not long to live, this wraith-like figure decided to see the world and so enrolled in a mechanic's course in Solihull for driving and servicing Landrovers. After advertising for a travelling companion, preferably another mechanic with brawn – he had the brains – they set off, with his outdated, non-refrigerated insulin rolling about in the back of the jeep, on what was to be the first of many journeys. These exhausting-even-for-the-healthy-man trips would often take years of tireless driving through Ethiopia, India, Singapore, Burma, Africa, Persia, Australia, America and Mexico. He crossed the Sahara Desert, lived in kraals in Africa and tents in India – once with three 'chattering soldiers' lying beside him until dawn, making sure that he wasn't going to 'rush over the border'. In Afghanistan he mistakenly bedded down on a camel route, only to be genially warned off by 'two of the most savage-looking people ... talking nineteen-to-the-dozen, with black beards and in rags and black turbans ... considering they could have knocked us on the head, it just shows what nice people they are'. Of his travelling companions, he was often less complimentary, complaining when one showed a 'distressing tendency to go to the best hotels, and sulks, if I say I won't'. High living was not the order of the day, although he once wrote home for 'grey flannel trousers with "facilities" to put a belt on to keep them up.......needed for looking tidy smart and going to embassies etc'. Throughout his travels, he was always taking photographs, and those of the Ethiopians and of the nomads in the Sahara are as beautiful as any that I have seen. Many were published in *National Geographic* magazine.

When arrested in Kenya, for what was thought to be a discrepancy in his identity papers, he told the police to ring the Queen of England. They did, and he was set free.

After his stepfather died and as the years passed, he and his mother became ever more reclusive, hiding away if anyone came to Ardgowan, and then only emerging to talk to one another, smoking like chimneys, and getting through some 400 'Senior Service' cigarettes a week. His royal visits went on as before.

In 1968, when his mother died, he moved from the grand surroundings of Ardgowan to a little cottage high on a hill nearby, overlooking the Firth of Clyde. Thereafter, when not on his travels, he lived a surreal double life of a courtier and hermit. Always dressed in the strangest attire, with a jersey on his head, which he called his 'cap of penitence', and with his legs through the arms of a purple V-neck that was tied with string around his waist, all finished off by mud-caked Wellington boots, he lived the life of a tinker. Sometimes thrown out of the local Greenock pubs for vagrancy, his days were otherwise spent passionately tending his garden and his nights reading gardening books.

It appears that it was he who inspired Prince Charles both to paint and to garden, for Denys was a horticultural wizard, who, despite his stick-like fragility, created a sumptuously cultivated swathe of garden out of the rocky Scots landscape. Azaleas grew in abundance, with purple irises and red primulas standing proud in long grass beside a stream. He also designed a great pergola of moss-covered tree trunks, entwining it with old roses, wisteria, honeysuckle and clematis. Substantially picturesque, it was the same size as his little 'Suicide Cottage', so called by Princess Margaret, who said that she would commit suicide if she had to be in it for more than half an hour. Inside, it was a riot of confusion; with seed packets watered by Denys, sprouting forth through the erupting eighteenth-century veneer of his tables. A nest of baby mice thrived on his pillow – just the pillow, as his pillowcases had all been eaten by the mice. As locals said, 'He was a wee bit dusky at times.'

Nothing, though, could stop the royal progress. When a visit was due, he would borrow clothes from anybody who would lend them – all his old clothes had also been eaten by the mice – and in minutes transform himself from vagrant to princeling. He would go down the hill to Ardgowan dressed as a tinker, and after sprucing himself up to the nines, would leave fit for the Queen, hair cut, washed, and shaved, and in his borrowed coat, suit and highly polished shoes, he was ready for his other life.

Such was Denys Dawnay's strange story. Marvelled at by all who knew him, he was a man of sadly unknown genius, and in his lifetime his work was seen only by his friends. Now, twenty-three years after his death, with the publication of *The House of Tekelden*, it is hoped that he will have thousands of new admirers.

STOMACH ABOVE EVERYTHING

THE HOUSE OF TEKELDEN

from 463 to the present day.

by

DENYS DAWNAY

TO FLOWER

In the almost certainly vain hope that the history of his ancestors will teach him to improve.

"He may do without books — what is knowledge but grieving?
He may do without hope — what is hope but deceiving?
He may do without love — what is passion but pining?
BUT WHERE IS THE RAT THAT CAN DO WITHOUT DINING?"

PREFACE

My thanks are due firstly to His Majesty the King, for graciously permitting me to reproduce the three Holbeins in the Collection at Windsor Castle; to Lord Durham, Mrs Lumpkins, Miss N. Kelly and Mr Edward Tail for allowing me to reproduce pictures in their possession; to the Trustees of the National Gallery, the National Portrait Gallery, the Tate Gallery, the Victoria and Albert Museum and the British Museum; and to the authorities of the Louvre and of the Rijksmuseum, Amsterdam for allowing me to reproduce pictures: and finally to Flower for allowing free access to the archives of the Tekelden family and for giving me permission to reproduce two of his pictures and also a page from his mother's scrap-book.

Denys Dawnay.
Ardgowan. February 1945.

CONTENTS

CHAPTER I
The Begining.

The Evolution of the Dachshund, according to Darwin, occurred in the following way: in the Jurassic Age a Brontosaurus (Pl. I.) sickening of its own kind, consorted with a prehistoric carniverous marsupial called a bandicoot or pig-rat (Pl. II. Fig. 1). The issue of this fearsome couple, was the first dachshund as we know the family today, called the Neanderthal Dachshund (Plate II, Fig 2). Darwin describes what this creature was like in his famous 'Origin of Species': "... covered with long matted hair, with a sloping forehead such as to allow but little brain, the creature was of horrible ferocity and had a certain low cunning. Its chief food was the breast of pterodactyls, but often it would eat the leathery wings the toothed beaks and even the claws. It was also fond of the fleshy part of the dinosaurs' foot."

Plate 1

Brontosauri in 40,000,000. B.C.

from a drawing by the author based on fossilized

skeletons in the Natural History Museum at

South Kensington.

Plate II

Fig. 1. Jurassic Bandicoot or Pig-Rat.

Fig. 2. The Neandertal Dachshund

from drawings by the author.

Fig. 1.

Fig. 2.

CHAPTER II
The Sack of Rome.

Rome was sacked by Alaric in 410, by the Vandals in 455; neither of these tragedies could compare with the Sack of Rome in 463 by RATTILA the HUND*, the Scourge of God as he was called. He is the ancestor of the Tekelden family. The atrocities he and his band of followers committed were truly fearful. They pillaged, burnt, murdered — did every concievable beastliness. The Romans after experiences of two previous sackings, were prepared for murder and robbery: but worse was to follow. In an old Roman chronicle of about 490, is the following dreadful passage: "Eheu!, eheu! oppugnato templo, Rattila suique virgines quae custodiebant Sacram Flammam, mormorderunt!" "Alas! Alas! Rattila and his followers attacked the temple and bit the virgins guarding the Sacred Flame!"

*"The Hund" or Hound, a shortened form of Dachshund.

Plate III

The Sack of Rome in 463 by Rattila.

from a modern colour – lithograph.

CHAPTER III
The Conquest.

From the Sack of Rome in the 5th century, there is absolutely no trace of the family for the next 600 years. Then, however we get the valuable evidence of the Bayeux Tapestry. I reproduce a section of it (Pl. iv.) illustrating the two brothers WILLIAM and LEWINE TEKELDEN in action at the battle of Hastings. Some of the family, on the strength of this, claim to be of Norman descent. But such is clearly not the case. In fact it is known that the Conqueror hired them to fight, on account of their great ferocity. This was a by-word in those times as may be seen from the Latin inscription: "Hic·fratres·horribili·Willelm et Lewine Teckelden". (Here are the horrible brothers, W. and L. Teckelden). After the Conquest William was given the job of helping to compile Domesday Book by making an inventory of all the butchers and pie-makers. He did this with the utmost efficiency! No more is known.

Plate IV

William and Lewine Tekelden in 1066. A section
of
The Bayeux Tapestry.

CHAPTER IV
The Knight.

Plate V is reproduced from a colour print published in 1820, representing RUPERT TEKELDEN and his wife BERENICE. It is based on information got from a bill dated 1215 to Rupert from an English armourer. The text of the bill runs as follows—
"For y-makynge cote of maille of fyhnst stele with oo gret longe corre for nosse ant y-spezhule pece for taille, lest this xuld ben y-loppid off in combatte, Squiere Rupert Ticklden, y-clept Squiere Squintlynge dius tu grote."

For readers unversed in medieval English, I append a translation: "For making (a) coat of mail of finest steel with a great long cover for (the) nose and (a) special piece for (the) tail, lest this should be lopped off in combat, Squire Rupert Tekelden, known as Squire Squintling, owes two groats". Another medieval poet informs us:

"He squintid in swich horibil waye
His wyf y-made hem wern his vizzor nihte ant daye."

4

Plate V

Rupert and Berenice Tekelden in 1215

From a Colour Print (published in 1820)
in the
British Museum.

CHAPTER V
The Gourmet

Plate VI. is a colour print (published 1820) based on a missing picture by Van Eyck. The original picture, painted about 1425, represented JAN TEKELDEN and his wife (name unknown) evidently in their later years, as just before he died, the poet Chaucer had written of this same Jan, in a narrative poem entitled "The Rat's Tail" (or Tale?)

"Take Jan the Rat, and fostre him wel with milk,
And tendre flesh, and make his couche of silk,
And lat him seen a by cucced in the hal;
Anon he weyveth milk, and flesh, and al,
And every deyntee of wich that I can talk;
Swich appetyt hath he for pys of porc."

There is little more information about Jan, except that as well as pies:

"Wel loved he garleek, oynons, and eek lekes,
And for to drinken strong wyn, reed as blood."

5

Plate VI

Jan Tekelden and his wife in 1425

From a Colour Print (published 1820)

British Museum.

CHAPTER VI
Beauty and —

Jan Tekelden had a son, RUDOLPH TEKELDEN, who married a French dachshund famous for her beauty called DIANE de MOUSIER (in about 1440) and they had a son who was called MAXIMILLIAN TEKELDEN who was the father of Odo (see the following chapter). Plate VII is the third of the colour prints of 1820, and shows an imaginery version of Diane and Maximillian in the clothes of 1450. Apart from her fame as a beauty, nothing much is known of them. It is sad that such a charming-looking little dachshund as Maximillian should have been the father of the dreadful Odo.

Plate VII

Diane de Mousier and Maximillian Tekelden in 1450.

From a Colour Print (published 1820)

British Museum.

CHAPTER VII
The Beast.

In the reproduction of Rüland Früauf the Younger's picture (Pl.viii) a figure dressed as a high dignitary of the church can be discerned. He is none other than ODO TEKELDEN, Cardinal Lord Archbishop of Bavaria, known as "Odo the Odious." With him are seen his brother's wife and her son (walking behind), as they lived with him (he not being married). The nephew, who was called Heinrich (see following chapter), was his uncle's sole heir.

There are few facts known of Odo's life, and how he became a Cardinal is a mystery. By some sort of trickery doubtless. It is known that he had a most horrible dungeon in his castle, full of instruments of torture such as paw-pressers, ear and nose-clippers and tail-twisters which made the tails of his victims like bits of barley-sugar. He also used to invite his rivals to dinner and give them Poisoned Pork Pies to eat! In front are walking his private bodyguard, armed with halberds — a necessary precaution for one so hated!

Plate VIII

Odo and Heinrich Tekelden in 1500.
by
Rüland Früauf the Younger

Monastery of Klosterneuberg

CHAPTER VIII
The Fool.

HEINRICH TEKELDEN was not a nice character inspite of being brought up in such an ecclesiastical atmosphere. To begin with he was intensely stupid, having only two thoughts in his head—his Stomach and his clothes (which are very beautiful, to judge by Holbein's fine portrait at Windsor*) In 1521 he got very excited when he heard of the Diet of Worms: though it did not <u>sound</u> very appetizing, he thought there must be something in it, as the Emperor Charles V (a great glutton) appeared to have invented it. When Heinrich eventually discovered that it was of a political rather than an edible nature, he was very huffy indeed. He married twice: firstly RATHILDA RITTER, and second KATHERINE PAW when much older. They had one son. The drawings of his two wives (Pl. x.) by Holbein at Windsor, are good examples of the draughtsmanship of that master.

*See Plate IX.

Plate IX

Heinrich Tekelden   in   1530.

by Hans Holbein

in the Collection of His Majesty the King

Windsor at Castle

HOLBEIN

Plate X

Rathilda Ritter and Katherine Paw in 1530

by Hans Holbein

in the Collection of H.M. the King

at Windsor Castle.

CHAPTER IX
The Courtier

Heinrich's son WALTER TEKELDEN came over to England when quite young and was remarked on for his beautiful manners (unlike a certain descendant of his) and for this reason was in high favour at Court. One day he saw the most beautiful of the Queen's Dachshunds-in-Waiting alight from her carriage, and make to cross the horrible muddy street. Quick as a flash he ran forward and spread his brand-new cloak at her feet for her to walk on. Needless to add that quite soon afterwards, she accepted his hand in marriage! Her name was PHŒBE FLOWER.

Queen Elizabeth was quite delighted by the whole affair, and she knighted him on his wedding day. Out of deference to her, he assumed by deed poll an English name and was known to all from that day to this as SIR WALTER RATEIGH. The Queen also lent them the royal manor of Ratfield for their honeymoon. Two charming pictures of them are reproduced: one a miniature by Nicholas Hillyarde (Pl.xi); the other a full length by Zucchero (Pl.xii)

Plate XI

Walter Tekelden in 1580

from a Miniature by Nicholas Hillyarde

in the Victoria and Albert Museum

Plate XII

Phœbe Flower in 1580

by Zucchero

in the Collection of Flower at Lambton

CHAPTER X
The Poet.

There is nothing remarkable to write of in PAULUS TEKELDEN's life. It was almost without incident. He was fond of the arts and there were always several poets and painters to be found at his house. He wrote some charming verses himself, usually to his wife, HENRIETTA GOLDRAT. Here is one of them:

"Her skin like gold did glister
(How I longed for what I saw!)
I trembled when I kiss'd her
Tiny little paw.
How could I resist her?
I tremble, quake and quail
To think I might have miss'd her
Little lizard-tail." *

The portraits of them (Pl. xiii) by Van Dyck (a frequent visitor to their house) are in the Louvre.

* See also Appendix I, page 25, for more poems by Paulus Tekelden.

Plate XIII

Paulus Tekelden and Henrietta Goldrat in 1620

by Van Dyck

in the Lourre

VAN DYCK

CHAPTER XI
The Painter.

But few words are needed to introduce their son. For he was none other than RATBRANDT TEKELDEN van RIJN, the world-famous painter. As is well-known, he lived in Holland, (on the river Rijn, hence his name) and married a dear little Flemish dachshund called RATSKIA van ULENBURGH.

The drawing here reproduced (Plate xiv) in the Rijksmuseum, Amsterdam, is of course a by Ratbrandt himself, being a self-portrait done in his studio, with his wife acting as model. He almost always did self-portraits (though one cannot understand why, with a face like that) and it is not surprising that he sold very few pictures in his life-time, and died very poor indeed.

Plate XIV

Ratbrandt Tekelden van Rijn and Ratskia van Ulenburgh

from a drawing by Ratbrandt (1645)

in the Rijksmuseum, Amsterdam.

CHAPTER XII
The Snob.

Being left nothing but debts by his father, CARL TEKELDEN determined somehow to regain sufficient money to live comfortably. So he began to toady and flatter everyone of any importance whom he met, hoping for some benefit from them. One of these happened to be Charles II, whilst he was still in exile. Carl did his utmost to be ingratiating to the Prince, thinking that some good must come of it, and also because he was the most horrible snob. After the Restoration, Carl came over to England, hoping to be made a duke at the least for "past services", and though of course this did not happen, the good-natured monarch did give him a little house at Kew as a wedding present when he married a little English dachshund called CATHERINE* His position now assured, his pride and arrogance asserted themselves with a vengeance. The poet, Alexander Pope, in a long poem, tells us to what lengths his snobbery went. He

*Catherine RATSTAYLE, last surviving member of an old English family.

would dress himself in the most flamboyant and fashionable clothes and strut round Kew Gardens and whenever he saw a dachshund in rather poorer and humbler circumstances than himself he would go up to him and, with his nose in the air, say:

"I am his Highness' dog at Kew:

Pray tell me, Sir, whose dog are you?"

with such a horribly disdainful expression, that the other little dog (who of course never had any grand connections), was dreadfully mortified and hurt.

He insisted of course on being painted by Lely (following the fashion as usual) and the two portraits of himself and his wife, reproduced opposite (Plate XV) are now in Flower's collection at Lambton.

LELY

CHAPTER XIII
The General.

What a contrast between father and son! Born in an age of soldiers and famous fighters. there was none so famous or so brilliant as FRIEDRICH CARL GUSTAVUS ADOLPHUS, Prinz von und zu ROTBLUME-STRINDELBERG, Herzog von PREUSSISCH-RATENKOPF-TEKELDEN, to mention just a few of his many titles, showered on him for his brilliant feats of arms. His victories over all adversaries are too well-known and too numerous to need repeating. One might just mention the famous battle of Ratillies in 1706 when he put to rout the great Duke of Marlborough himself. "An army", said this famous dachshund in an order of the day, "marches on its Stomach", and on the strength of this he made it a rule, never to start a day's fighting (or any other day for that matter) without first reinforcing himself with a treble ration of food (usually pork-pies, a great delicacy to him). He married EMMA von BIRKENSCHLOSS in 1700. (See Pl. xvi).

Plate XVI

The Duke of Preussisch-Ratenkopf-Tekelden and his wife, Emma von Birkenschloss in 1700 by Kneller, in the National Portrait Gallery.

CHAPTER XIV
The Musician.

From the realities of war to the pleasures of peace! The world of 1730 was a world of pleasure-seeking, of rustic simplicity, of merry-making and laughter; a world whose peace was disturbed only by the pattering of dancing paws on the velvet-textured lawns and the strains of a mandolin. The world of the fête champêtre in fact. Into this world the son of the great general, ANTOINE TEKELDEN flung himself with all the enthusiasm of youth. He met a charming Rumanian dachshund called TILLI MIMESCU and her sister Tootoo. The two sisters used to dance and sing whilst he played his lute. They used to have the most lovely picnics and make garlands of roses to put in their hair. Although very fond of both, he really liked Tilli the best and so he married her. But Tootoo always lived with them. (See Plate xvii. where is reproduced Lancret's beautiful picture of the three of them).

Plate XVII

Antoine Tekelden and Tilli Mimesen and her sister Tootoo

From the painting by Nicolas Lancret (1730). in

the Wallace Collection

CHAPTER XV
The Actor.

After a childhood spent in such a setting, it is hardly surprising that that their son, DAVID TEKELDEN should have had a leaning towards the arts. When still quite young he went to England and went onto the stage. In due course he became one of the most famous actors in the world. He acted under the stage name of DAVID RATTICK. He naturally came into contact with MRS SARAH SIDDONIA, the famous actress, and eventually he got engaged to her, and they were married. The two reproductions of Zoffany's well-known pictures (Plates xviii and xix) in the possession of Lord Durham, show the two, entertaining friends at Shakespeare's temple at Hampton. The third reproduction, (Plate xx) is of Gainsborough's portrait of Sarah, in the National Gallery, London. Perhaps the best-known of any picture in the world. Gainsborough had great difficulty in the painting of

the head. He had to scrape it out and repaint it a dozen times—
and finally he lost his temper: "Damn your nose, Madam", he
said, "theres no end to it." (Of course he meant that there was
no end to the painting of it). Now if there was one thing that
Sarah was touchy about, it was about the length of her nose (and
to tell the truth, although fairly short for a dachshund, it did, all
the same, exceed the dimensions required by strict classical
cannons of beauty.   Trembling with fury at this remark
she rose from her seat and left the studio, never more to go
back. Out of pique she went straight off to Sir Joshua Rey-
nolds' studio and was painted by him instead. Sir Joshua's
picture, which is now in America, is entitled, "Mrs Siddonia
as the Tragic Mouse" which only goes to show how much it
had gone to her heart, the whole unlucky incident.

Plate XIX

David Rattiek and his wife at Hampton

From the painting by John Zoffany

in the Collection of the Earl of Durham

Plate XX

Mrs Siddonia

from the painting by Thomas Gainsborough

in the National Gallery.

THOMAS GAINSBOROUGH

CHAPTER XVI
The Lover.

The Ratticks made a good deal of money from their acting, and their son, LUDOVIC TEKELDEN was able to live a very pleasant, comfortable life. The picture here reproduced (Pl.xxi) is now in the Wallace Collection.   When he was just grown up, he was just commencing the "grand tour" of Europe, when he met in Paris a little dachshund famed throughout all the world for her beauty. Her name was HÉLÈNE, Princesse de TROYE,* or "la Ratte Ravissante" as Marie-Antoinette used to call her. She was as good and aimiable as she was beautiful. She would like to spend most of the day in her beautiful garden close to Versailles, meditating. After an hour or so's thought, she would murmer "l'Amour, toujours l'Amour" or some such charming sentiment in her delicious abstracted voice, and would then fall into a reverie once more. Ludovic married her and they lived in Paris until the Revolution, when they managed to escape to England.
*See Plate xxii.

Plate XXI

Ludovic Tekelden in 1790

from the painting by Jean Honoré Fragonard

in the Wallace Collection.

Plate XXII

Hélène, Princesse de Troye   in 1790

from a contemporary colour print

in the Victoria and Albert Museum.

CHAPTER XVII
The Rake

With two such charming parents, one would have thought that FLUSH TEKELDEN would have inherited some of their good points. Alas! such was not the case. He was pretentious, avaricious — and dreadfully greedy. He gambled away vast sums of money at cards and was known amongst his contemporaries as Flash Flush of Querns. (Querns was the name of his house near Bath). In the reproduction (Pl.xxiii) from a print by H. Alken, he is to be seen driving his tandem at reckless speed round the park at Querns.

He married firstly the famous MADAME RATTIER, who held a salon in Paris, where all the wit of Europe was to be found Her portrait by David (Pl.xxiv) is one of the glories of the Louvre, though actually it is unfinished. She discovered David had been going to a rival's salon, and after this she refused to go on sitting. (This may account for the rather huffy expression in her eye). Flush married her on account of her celebrity, and not for love, and when he discovered that she only enjoyed lying on the sofa and being witty, and utterly declined to go into the kitchen and make him his favourite dish, pork pies, his rage knew no bounds and he drove the poor little thing out of the house. Indeed his passion for pork pies was the chief thing in his life. "A dachshund can jog along on 40,000 pork pies a year" was a notorious saying of his.

For several years he hunted about for a wife (Madame Rattier having died) who would combine the two virtues of being able to cook pies and be sufficiently wealthy to be able to support him, for his gambling and hard living had made heavy inroads into his money. In 1840 he discovered the very person MAY ELIZABETH von RATSCHILD,* a daughter of the great banking house. How she regretted the day she married!

He was quite beastly to her, making her cook all day and all night and spending her money. It was a happy release for her when he died, shortly afterwards, of a surfeit of pork pies.

* See Plate xxv.

Plate XXIV

Madame Rattier in 1820

from the painting by Louis David

in the Louvre

DAVID

Plate XXV

May Elizabeth von Ratschild in 1840

from a contemporary Watercolour

in the Collection of Miss Nelly Kelly of Lambton

Castle, Co. Durham.

CHAPTER XVIII
The Good Cook.

Fortunately, ERNEMAN TEKELDEN inherited few of his father's vices, except that he too was insatiably greedy and also adored pork pies. Like his father, he married not for love, but because JUDURKA SÜSS was such an excellent cook But she was terribly conceited and sometimes in order to snub her, he would remind her of his reason for marrying her:

"I could not love thee, dear so much,
Loved I not pork pies more"
he used to tell her with rather brutal frankness.

The portrait of them by Whistler, is too little known. It was exhibited at the Royal Society in 1840, under the title of "Symphony in Black and Grey", and "Symphony in Lilac and Green." (Plate xxvi)

Plate XXVI

Erneman Tekelden and Judurka Süss in 1840

also entitled "Symphony in Black and Grey", and "Symphony

in Lilac and Green"

from the paintings by James McNeill Whistler

in the Collection of Edward Tail, Esq. of Lambton Castle.

WHISTLER

CHAPTER XIX
The Slanderer.

JUNKER JAN was the name of Erneman's son. He was a dachshund of a modest, retiring disposition, enjoying simple country pursuits such as hunting: he hated anything to do with the busy glittering bustle of Edwardian society. In 1904 he married (unfortunately) MARY BETZYAM who was opposite to him in every way being vivacious, malicious, witty, loving to be surrounded by masses of people, loving London, hating the country. Poor "J.J." (as he was called) had a difficult life, though they both conformed to the dictum of "keeping up appearances" and all the world imagined them to be a model married couple. The hardest blow of all fell, when Mary published an extraordinarily libellous book of memoires about all her (and his) friends which brought with it a blaze of notoriety and scandal most obnoxious to J.J. The book was called "Tales I have told, and Tails I have seen."　　Their pictures, by Sargent, are in the Tate. (Pl.xxvii)

Plate XXVII

Junker Jan Tekelden and Mary Betzam

in 1904

from the paintings by John Singer Sargent

in the Collection of Mrs Elizabeth Lumpkins of Lambton Castle.

SARGENT

CHAPTER XX
The Highbrow.

Junker Jan's son was called "J.J. Junior". His real name was JEREMY JEM TEKELDEN. He married an Italian dachshund called FRIVOLE, Marchesa de CATHERISE. She was not so much beautiful as striking to look at. She was also very, very highbrow (belying her name) only enjoying the most advanced kind of art and literature. Under her influence J.J. junior also became exceedingly highbrow and he once went as far as to say that only fools liked representational art. In any case he refused to be painted by anyone but Picasso (Plate xxviii) Although this does not perhaps give a precise idea of his appearance, it is certainly a work of art of great merit. Frivole herself was painted by Augustus John (Plate xxviii). It is one of the artist's best-known portraits. Both pictures are in the Tate.

Plate XXVIII

Jeremy Jem Tekelden and Frivole de Catherise

from the paintings by Pablo Picasso and

Augustus John, in the Tate Gallery.

PICASSO

A. JOHN

CHAPTER XXI
The Catastrophe.

And so we come to the birth of FLOWER. I merely state this melancholy fact, baldly and without comment. Other books have been written about him*, and doubtless more are still to come, and I do not intend to sully the pages of this book with any description of him whatever. Many are in possession of the facts, and for those who are not, their ignorance is bliss. All his characteristics seem to be derived from William, Odo, Heinrich, Carl and Flush of Querns. And from his grand-mother, Mary Betzyam. His physical appearance seems to have been inherited from Rupert, whose wife made him wear his vizor night and day, so horribly did he squint. Alas that there are no vizors nowadays! Plate xxix is a page from his mother's scrap-book. Indeed a catastrophic event!

*
See "Flower and the Flowers" by the same author.

THE END.

Plate XXIX

A page from Frivole de Catherise's scrap-book

at the time of the birth of Flower.